NOT THE F

"NOT THE BEST LOOKING BIRD"

The wit and wisdom of Ian Holloway

Compiled by Grant Tucker

\Bb\
Biteback Publishing

First published in Great Britain in 2011 by
Biteback Publishing Ltd
Westminster Tower
3 Albert Embankment
London
SE1 7SP
Copyright © Grant Tucker 2011

ISBN 978-1-84954-169-5

10 9 8 7 6 5 4 3 2 1

A CIP catalogue record for this book is available from the
British Library.

Set in Bookman Old Style and Round Slab Serif
Front cover photograph © Getty Images Ltd.

Printed and bound in Great Britain by
CPI Group (UK) Ltd, Croydon, CR0 4YY

FOREWORD

Over the last decade Ian 'Ollie' Holloway has become a household name, thanks to his quick wit, unorthodox wisdom and an outrageous temper. He is never one to mince his words and the media know that Ollie will always speak his mind. But he isn't just a man with the gift of the gab; he is also a quality football manager.

Ollie has lived and breathed football since he was picked to join Bristol Rovers aged nine. He went on to play for several clubs and made over 600 professional appearances, scoring forty-nine goals. But it wasn't until he became manager of Bristol Rovers in 1996 that he gained real prominence for his infamous rants. Since then he has managed QPR, Plymouth Argyle, Leicester City and more recently oversaw the promotion and relegation of Blackpool. However, Ollie also has a different side to him. He is a loving father of four children, devoted husband of twenty-four years and passionate campaigner on deaf issues.

This book gathers together all of Ollie's best known remarks and has uncovered some hidden gems. I know you will have as much fun reading this book as I did compiling it. Enjoy!

Grant Tucker
London, July 2011

HOLLOWAY FACTFILE

Full name: Ian Scott Holloway
Born: Kingswood, Bristol, 2 March 1963
Siblings: John, Sue
Education: Sir Bernard Lovell School
Married: Kim, May 1987
Children: William, Eve, Chloe, Harriet

CAREER TIMELINE

1963: Ian Scott Holloway is born in Bristol, England on 12 March 1963.
1974: Holloway goes to Sir Bernard Lovell School; he was in the same class as future professional footballer Gary Penrice and they remain good friends.
1981: In the spring, Holloway turns professional at Bristol Rovers as a midfielder.
1985: After four seasons at Bristol Rovers he transfers to Wimbledon.
1986: Brentford buys Holloway for £25,000.
1987: Holloway has a brief spell at Torquay United, playing just five games. He returns to Bristol Rovers in the summer.
1991: The new manager of Queens Park Rangers, Gerry Francis, signs up Holloway for £230,000.
1996: Once again, Holloway returns to Bristol Rovers, this time as a player-manager.

1999: Holloway's last year as a professional player; he retires from the pitch to concentrate fully on the management of Rovers.

2001: Holloway appointed manager of QPR, with the aim of keeping them in Division One. Sadly Holloway cannot turn around their fortunes and they are relegated.

2004: QPR are promoted back into The Championship.

2006: After speculation that Holloway was to become manager at Leicester City, QPR suspend him. In fact Holloway becomes manager of Plymouth Argyle on 28 June.

2007: Once again, speculation arises regarding the vacant managerial position at Leicester City. This time the rumour proves correct and Holloway leaves Plymouth to manage Leicester City.

2008: Following Leicester City's relegation Holloway leaves the club.

2009: After nearly a year out of football Holloway is announced as Blackpool's new manager.

2010: In his first full season, he leads Blackpool to promotion to the Premier League.

2011: After just one season in the Premier League Blackpool are relegated, returning to The Championship.

"I DON'T SEE THE PROBLEM WITH FOOTBALLERS TAKING THEIR SHIRTS OFF AFTER SCORING A GOAL. THEY ENJOY IT AND THE YOUNG LADIES ENJOY IT TOO. I SUPPOSE THAT'S ONE OF THE MAIN REASONS WOMEN COME TO FOOTBALL GAMES, TO SEE THE YOUNG MEN TAKE THEIR SHIRTS OFF OF COURSE THEY'D HAVE TO GO AND WATCH ANOTHER GAME BECAUSE MY LADS ARE AS UGLY AS SIN."

On the new rule restricting footballers from removing their shirts during a match.

"We need a big, ugly defender. If we had one of them we'd have dealt with County's first goal by taking out the ball, the player and the first three rows of seats in the stands."

After a defeat by Notts County.

"Apparently it's my fault that the *Titanic* sank."

On criticism from Plymouth Argyle fans during Leicester City's match against their team.

"I'd rather do that than build chicken sheds no one wanted!"

On Blackpool making the Championship play-off final in 2010, Holloway having spent a year out of football making hen houses.

"To put it in gentleman's terms, if you've been out for a night and you're look-ing for a young lady and you pull one, some weeks they're good looking and some weeks they're not the best. Our perfor-mance today would have been not the best looking bird but at least we got her in the taxi. She weren't the best looking lady we ended up taking home but she was very pleasant and very nice, so thanks very much, let's have a coffee."

On the 'ugly' win against Chesterfield.

"In football you need to have everything in your cake mix to make the cake taste right. One little bit of ingredient that Tony uses in his cake that gets talked about all the time is Rory's throw. Call that cinnamon and he's got a cinnamon-flavoured cake. It's not fair and it's not right and it's only a small part of what he does."

On Tony Pulis's style of management.

"Sir David Beckham? You're having a laugh. He's just a good footballer with a famous bird. Can you imagine if Posh was called Lady Beckham? We'd never hear the end of it!"

On rumours of a possible knighthood for David Beckham.

"Why haven't they got cameras? The officials can speak to each other easily enough now. Why aren't we using laptops that are linked up and can give a decision in five seconds? A chimpanzee could do it – with not much training. We might as well go back to being cavemen, grab our girl by the hair, drag her into the cave whether she wants to come in or not because we may as well live in that age. We've come forward, haven't we?"

On goal-line technology.

"If he's only worth £4 million, then I'm a Scotsman called McTavish."

"Dream on! If they want to insult me by only offering £3.5 million and then get it all over the paper and try to upset me well, sorry, they're barking up the wrong tree, they're messing with the wrong dog and I'll come and bite them."

On bids received for captain Charlie Adam.

"Sometimes you have to work for what you want. I did, and my dad did – in a foundry, living in a council house. It didn't do him any harm... Charlie will go down in folk history too, and I might even start carving a statue of him myself. Someone give me a penknife and some wood."

On Charlie Adam staying put.

"We haven't got undersoil heating, so the club has brought in something that looks like it should be in a fairground. It's some kind of generator that blows heat on to the pitch... I waited behind it for ten minutes thinking I could get myself a hot dog."

On Bloomfield Road.

"Man love? Man flu I've heard of. Let's just get this straight, no no no don't go there. Let's just get this straight... On a looks front my wife's got a lot more about her than H but on a managerial front he takes some beating."

Holloway when asked if there was any man love between him and 'Arry Redknapp.

"If Alex Ferguson is being bullied by a player and his agent, how wrong is the game? They say it's not fair on the player. Rubbish. The player has had his wages every week. They bought him, they worked with him, he belongs to them. It's so obvious."

On Wayne Rooney's transfer fiasco.

"I told him what a cracking lady his mum was and how much we all miss her and how proud I am of him and his brother. Because I'm a common bloke and he reminds me of an ordinary bloke you'd meet in the street... I told him to leave our women alone tonight if he goes out!"

Wise advice for Prince William ahead of a stag do in Blackpool.

"'You'll Never Walk Alone' is one of my dad's favourite songs; he's no longer with us and I was singing it with them."

Holloway explains why he sang along with the Liverpool fans when he took Blackpool to Anfield.

"I remember I had this argument at school one day. I was hit by a bigger kid and I came home and Dad said, 'What was that all about then?' And I said, 'Well, I said something about him.' And Dad said, 'Oh, never talk about people, son, talk *to* people.'"

"My dad taught me life is about people, it 'aint about where you come from or who you are. You should be able to stand in a room and talk to anybody, learn from everybody and love them for who they are."

Father to son advice.

"IT'S BEEN AN ABSOLUTE LIVING NIGHTMARE, TO BE HONEST. IT IS JUST LUDICROUS; I DON'T SEE WHO IT BENEFITS AT ALL. WHEN MY WIFE'S SHOPPING, WE NEED SOME MILK AND BREAD ON A REGULAR BASIS. WE CAN'T BUY IT ALL AT THE START AND THEN WAIT UNTIL JANUARY BECAUSE IT WOULD HAVE ALL GONE OFF"

On the January transfer window. That's that pretty much summed up then.

"I love Blackpool. We're very similar. We both look better in the dark."

On Blackpool.

"Hasney's bust his hooter. He can smell round corners now."

On an injury sustained by central defender Hasney Aljofree.

"There's only one word for me: pride. We needed to play well and we did against a fantastic side and you can see the improvement my club has made. We believe in ourselves again. We've had a little wobble but there's a few games to play yet."

Holloway congratulates Blackpool after a 1–1 draw at Tottenham.

"We got it mixed up. I wanted to take Varney off and put Carney on but we ended up taking off Crainey. It all got confused. Varney, Carney, Crainey is a tongue-twister. We made a mistake but I'll let my staff off as they're great."

Hollway tries his hand at tongue-twisters.

"If the player hadn't gone missing we'd have had David Nugent. With twenty minutes to go we had Nugent signed on, but no one could locate him, so he couldn't sign his contract and it all fell through. So that's one that wriggled out of the net. But it happens. It wasn't possible to get a back-up with twenty minutes left. Should I have had to worry about that? Not really, I don't think. These rules are stupid. They should be banned."

On the strict transfer deadline day rules.

"I heard Michel Platini was coming to our friendly game in Latvia the other night, but unfortunately I couldn't find him, which is just as well for him because I'd love a word about the rules!"

On UEFA President, Michel Platini.

"It absolutely fills you with pride to see how people's whole lives are lifted by what their football team is doing. It is just quite amazing."

On the fans.

"If that's not a penalty on Luke Varney then deary, deary me. Rafael makes no effort to play the ball at all, he wipes the player out, and it's a stonewaller. If we go 3–0 up, who knows? Saying that, what a team United are. The players they brought on, the way they came strong at the end: they are a magnificent team. And my Blackpool aren't a million miles away from them, I'm telling you."

Holloway gracious in defeat.

"YOU ARE TALKING OUT OF YOUR HAT. I WOULD LIKE TO SAY OUT OF YOUR ASS, BUT THAT'S A DONKEY AND I DON'T LIKE HAVING A GO AT DONKEYS. IF SOME BRIGHT SPARK FROM THE PREMIER LEAGUE, OR BARCLAYS PREMIER LEAGUE AS WE'RE SUPPOSED TO CALL IT, WANTS TO COME DOWN AND HAVE A CHAT AND A CUP OF COFFEE ... YOU'LL PROBABLY GET IT CHUCKED IN YOUR LAP."

"I said, 'What time do you call this? You're twenty minutes late and if you were a player waiting for my bus, we'd be gone. You're not that important.' He went, 'I was doing something else,' and I said, 'Well, I'm not happy with that, where's your tie?' I took my tie off and walked the other way past him and he said, 'Where are you going now?' and I said, 'I'm going to buy a cappuccino because I've heard you're as tight as a duck's backside.'"

Holloway recalls his interview with Karl Oyston for the Blackpool Manager job.

"This is a massive game for us – this is life-changing. This will change my players' lives. It will change the face of this club for ever. If we get £90 million... It is obscene me even saying it when people are starving in the world. And yet that is the world we live in and that is where football is."

On the Championship play-off final 2010.

"I couldn't be more chuffed if I were a badger at the start of the mating season."

Holloway after QPR beat Cardiff.

"To the people who booed – boo to you!"

On Arsenal fans booing Blackpool players.

"When my mum was running our house, when I was a kid, all the money was put into tins. She knew what was in every tin and I know how much I've got in my tin – that's the way we'll run this club."

On QPR's financial management.

"Paul Furlong is my vintage Rolls-Royce and he cost me nothing. We polish him, look after him and I have him fine-tuned by my mechanics. We take good care of him because we have to drive him every day, not just save him for weddings."

On veteran striker Paul Furlong.

"There was a woman in it who was quite well-endowed and two boys who used to get drunk and have a fight – it had every-thing for me."

On Dukes Of Hazzard.

"He's a complete fruitcake, that bloke, isn't he? We've got to be careful with him, he's after the old crazy mantle and he's going to win it hands down."

On Stephen Ireland.

"He is the oldest swinger in town but at this level he will add a touch of class."

On veteran midfielder Teddy Sheringham.

"MY LADS HAVE MADE A HUGE DIFFERENCE TO THIS AREA ALREADY. WE HAVE RAISED AN AWFUL LOT OF MONEY FOR BRIAN HOUSE, A HOSPICE CHARITY HERE. WE WENT IN AND MET ALL THE PEOPLE THERE WHO AREN'T AS FORTUNATE AS US, GAVE UP CHRISTMASES TO GO AND STAND IN A SHOPPING MALL. SOME OF US DRESSED UP AS WOMEN. NOT ME. I WAS A PENGUIN."

On Blackpool FC's local work.

"I want to try and spread the support with my Bristol connection. Rovers are in the bottom division so why can't I try and convert some of them into Argyle fans? We're in the West Country so it's not that far away. Only two and a half hours away in a slow car, an hour and a half in a fast one – or ten minutes in a rocket! As long as you aimed it right, you'd be down here really quickly. Don't land it on the pitch, though, because you'd ruin it!"

On new fans.

"You can say that strikers are very much like postmen: they have to get in and out as quick as they can before the dog starts to have a go."

On strikers.

"I reckon the ball was travelling at 400mph, and I bet it burned the keeper's eyebrows off."

On Paul Furlong's free kick after a QPR victory over Crewe.

"Toad of Toad Hall?"

On then Chelsea manager Avram Grant.

"It's all very well having a great pianist playing but it's no good if you haven't got anyone to get the piano on the stage in the first place, otherwise the pianist would be standing there with no bloody piano to play."

After being criticised for using defensive players in midfield.

"I've got every right to do what I like. Who the hell are they to tell me my players are not good enough?"

Holloway on the £25,000 fine incurred after he made ten changes for a midweek game.

"We want women to come to football don't we? I think they're bloody pretty – a damn sight prettier than any bloke I've seen."

"You talk to women about footballers and what do they like – they like legs – and our shorts are getting longer. We should go back to the days when half your arse was hanging out."

On women and football.

"Whoever that was, I'd like to pull his pants down and slap him on the arse like I used to do to my kids. Apparently I'm not even allowed to do that anymore otherwise I'll have the health and safety on to me giving it the old 'hello'."

On the reporter who claimed QPR defender Danny Shittu would be sold.

"I rung Kenny Jackett straight away to congratulate him on getting Swansea promoted and he said, 'I'm waiting to get my goalie out of jail.' You can't even celebrate these days, can you?"

On celebrating.

"This is our cave, and I like living in it."

On staying at Loftus Road.

"Do you believe everything you read in *The Sun*? They've got some nice tits in that paper."

On being linked with the Millwall job.

"I got them from my father who had more sayings than you can hang your hat on!"

Holloway explains where he gets his sayings from.

"YOU NEVER COUNT YOUR CHICKENS BEFORE THEY HATCH. I USED TO KEEP PARAKEETS AND I NEVER COUNTED EVERY EGG THINKING I WOULD GET ALL EIGHT BIRDS. YOU JUST HOPED THEY CAME OUT OF THE NEST BOX LOOKING ALL RIGHT. I'M LIKE A SWAN AT THE MOMENT. I LOOK FINE ON TOP OF THE WATER BUT UNDER THE WATER MY LITTLE LEGS ARE GOING MAD."

"It's as if we've picked up the *Titanic* from the bottom of the ocean, turned it round and pointed it in the right direction."

On the good fortune of QPR.

"He's been out for a year and Richard Langley is still six months away from being Richard Langley and I could do with a fully fit Richard Langley."

On Richard Langley's rehabilitation.

"When the water stands still in the pond, it starts to stink."

On axing players from the squad.

"What we've all got to do is pick him up, slap him around and make him feel welcome."

On helping Doudou's homesickness.

"I had finished all the anger management lessons but I might get on the phone and book a few more!"

Holloway after getting sent off against Tranmere.

"When we seemed to be dying, we were a carcass and the vultures came and fed off our bones."

On players being sold while the club was in administration.

"Now I'm a little fella as it happens, but when I was really small I was nothing."

Holloway: quite short.

"Look at the prickly little fella down the road at Chelsea. He wants to win everything and we can learn from that. If there were two flies crawling up the wall he'd be desperate to back the winner."

Battling Chelsea.

"I mean no respect to Donatella. I'm sure she would not be flattered to hear she looks like Marc Bircham."

On Donatella Versace.

"THE WORLD'S GONE MAD. TONY BLAIR WON THE ELECTION, SO WHY'S HE GOTTA RESIGN? I THINK THE CONSERVATIVE FELLA SHOULD. IF HE COULDN'T WIN AN ELECTION WITH A FAILING GOVERNMENT, OR A FLAILING GOVERNMENT, WHAT'S THE MATTER WITH HIM? GET OUT, YOU AIN'T NO GOOD. I KNOW WE'RE NOT TALKING FOOTBALL... WE ARE, AREN'T WE?"

"Well a few of them have had their hair done."

On the effect Sky TV cameras would have on the players.

"I've got to get Dan Shittu ready for the Stoke game. I've told him to go to Iceland and ask if he can sit in one of their freezers."

Holloway on Dan Shittu's injury.

"I'm the only person getting angry at the anger management guy!"

Holloway on his anger management classes.

"The club isn't on solid ground – it's like I'm on a block of ice. I don't know whether I'm going to go through it or slide off."

On the state of QPR.

"Gareth Ainsworth is the most physical winger I've seen. He calls himself the wolf man because of his sideburns but I don't pick fault with hairdos if players perform."

On Gareth Ainsworth.

"It's like putting a snake in a bag: if you do not tie it up, it will wriggle free."

On rescuing a point against Millwall.

"I call him Ronseal, he does exactly what it says on the tin. He's an out-and-out winger. He can turn, he can beat people and he makes the right choice nearly every time."

On Jerome Thomas.

"He over-elaborated with his celebration
– he looked like a chicken stick."

*On Richard Langley's goal celebration at
Blackpool.*

"You have to ask about a bar of soap at this club. I even had to pay for our pre-match meal on my own credit card on Saturday."

"When you play with wingers you look a bit like a taxi with both doors open – anyone can get in or out."

"It's been a fight all the way along to get proper provision for the girls, especially a good education. There's been rows, tribunals, appeals and endless phone calls. We have been labelled as bolshie parents. My view is that every child in the world has the right to be educated properly and whether your eyes or ears don't work is irrelevant. But the system at the moment makes if difficult."

On the difficulty of raising deaf children.

"Most of our fans get behind us and are fantastic. But those who don't should shut the hell up or they can come round to my house and I will fight them."

On abusive chanting directed at the team during a home game.

"He's a big lad, he can clean out your guttering without standing on a ladder."

On Georges Santos.

"Everyone calls him a gypsy but I can assure you he doesn't live in a caravan. He has a house with foundations."

On QPR defender Gino Padula.

"In football, there is no definite lifespan or time span for a manager. After a while you start smelling of fish. The other week it looked like I was stinking of halibut!"

On QPR's bad start to the 2004/05 season.

"This is the people's club and everybody can have a piece of that pie – a pie that's already smelling beautifully."

On Queens Park Rangers.

"Not enough to go to brothels."

When asked how much he earned as a player, compared to Rooney.

"Who would have thought a few weeks ago that we would be sitting in this position now? It's like the song, 'wait a minute, it stopped hailing, guys are swimming, gals are sailing'. I love that song."

On being in the top ten.

"I was up and down like Zebedee from the *Magic Roundabout.*"

On QPR coming back from two down to beat Leicester 3–2.

"We had a monster team out there, all the big guys, the roof inspectors as I call them."

On the height of QPR's defence against Leicester.

"My day didn't start very well, the Holloway household was very sad this morning, we had to have our dog put down unfortunately but that's life. I've just said to the lads, you're born and you die on a date, you've got to work on the dash in the middle."

On living life.

"Everyone was laughing because if that was not a penalty then what was? I think my wife even saw that and she's down in St Albans listening to the radio!"

On the denied penalty at Grimsby.

"As far as I'm concerned, I'm from Bristol and so is that lad, and he got it wrong."

On the linesman not giving the foul for City's first goal.

"IF YOU CAN KEEP YOUR NOSES IN FRONT AT THE END, THAT'S WHAT COUNTS. IT'S BEEN SAID THAT I HAVE A BIT OF A ROMAN NOSE AND I AM KEEPING IT AHEAD AT THE MOMENT. HOPEFULLY IT'S ALL ABOUT THE LENGTH OF YOUR HOOTER BECAUSE I MIGHT BE IN FRONT AT THE END OF THE SEASON AS WELL!"

On QPR's dodgy start to the 2003/04 season.

"The doctor grafted a bit of Danny's hamstring onto his knee, but that won't be a problem for him, he's got more hamstring than the rest of the squad put together."

On Danny Shittu.

"The fat lady might be picking the mic up but I can't hear her singing yet."

"If is a big word. If I had long hair I could be a rock star."

When asked if Tony Thorpe's chance at Bristol City had gone.

"I've had a week from hell, I'm trying to learn how to relax. I'm now going to enjoy this, take my brain out and stick it in an ice bucket."

"IT'S LIKE WHEN I WAS A KID WAITING FOR SANTA TO TURN UP, WORRIED WHETHER I'D BEEN GOOD ENOUGH, TO THEN SEE HE HAS AND HE'S GIVEN YOU A FEW TOYS – THIS IS EVEN BETTER THAN THAT FEELING. THAT EXCITEMENT AND EXHILARATION WHEN YOU OPEN THE DOOR AND CAN SEE THE PRESENTS – THIS IS EVEN BETTER THAN THAT."

On the thrill of gaining promotion.

"I don't want to be patient – I want promotion this season."

"As a club, we are out of hospital now and we are looking forward to the convalescence and being fighting fit for the future."

On QPR coming out of administration.

"There's going to be one almighty run-in at the end – one almighty sprint for the post. We've got sixteen games to go now and I'd say that's about 500 yards of the 'race' to go. It's going to be one hell of a battle. It's going to be ugly."

On the promotion race.

"If the club was a chocolate bar, it would have licked itself."

On QPR's days in the Premiership.

"We've got to be solid and horrible to break down, I don't want to be southern softies!"

On QPR's attitude.

"I know everyone screams that he should play in the middle and I'm no nugget! I know what job he can do there."

On playing Richard Langley in a central role.

"We're no longer the flitty farty QPR."

On QPR's resilient attitude of late.

"I want you to bad rash them."

During his Radio Five live pre-match teamtalk.

"I was lucky enough to work with Gerry Francis for nearly ten years at two different clubs. Until I met him I thought I knew a lot about football. After I met him I knew nothing."

"Have you ever seen *The Incredibles*? They have a a kid and he's just so quick, like 'WOOSH' and he's gone, and they call him 'Dash'."

On Scott Sinclair, then on loan at Argyle.

"When my wife first saw Marc for the first time, she said he was a fine specimen of a man. She says I have nothing to worry about, but I think she wants me to buy her a QPR shirt with his name on the back for Christmas."

On QPR's new Danish striker Marc Nygaard.

"It was lucky that the linesman wasn't stood in front of me as I would have poked him with a stick to make sure he was awake."

Holloway states his opinion about the linesman's performance in a game against Bristol City.

"If you're a burglar, it's no good poncing about outside somebody's house, looking good with your swag bag ready. Just get in there, burgle them and come out. I don't advocate that obviously, it's just an analogy."

"I've got to knock that horrible smell out of my boys, because they smell of complacency."

"In the first-half we were like the Dog and Duck, in the second-half we were like Real Madrid. We can't go on like that. At full-time I was at them like an irritated Jack Russell."

"Every dog has its day, and today is woof day! Today I just want to bark!"

Holloway after securing promotion to the Championship.

"Bristol City came in first and all they talked about was 'how brilliant I was gonna be and when you're sixteen we'll give you this, and when you're seventeen we'll give you that, and when you're twenty-one you'll play for us and you'll never have to buy another pair of boots Mr Holloway. In fact here is his size right now.' And out they go. And in come Bristol Rovers and all the fella says is 'you did alright today, you were quite fair. Now if you want to be a good player son, you've got to want it more than the next fella and all we are guaranteeing you is you got to work hard, you got to be dedicated and it's down to you and it's down to you how good you can be. We know you might have a chance, but it's down to you son.' Now, who do you think I chose? I chose the people who told me the truth. I wasn't a big head, I knew what it was all about – you gotta work hard – mould yourself into something."

Holloway explains why he choose Bristol Rovers as a young boy.

"I am a football manager. I can't see into the future. Last year I thought I was going to Cornwall on my holidays but I ended up going to Lyme Regis."

Asked whether QPR would be able to beat Manchester City.

"It's like the film *Men in Black*. I walk around in a black suit, white shirt and black tie where I've had to flash my white light every now and again to erase some memories, but I feel we've got hold of the galaxy now. It's in our hands."

Holloway on QPR's financial situation.

"I always say that scoring goals is like driving a car. When the striker is going for goal, he's pushing down that accelerator, so the rest of the team has to come down off that clutch. If the clutch and the accelerator are down at the same time, then you are going to have an accident."

"They will be relieved if we lose and get relegated. Then I am not badgering them."

On the Premier League's alleged desire to see Blackpool relegated.

"It will be the end of the world."

On the prospect of relegation.

"Brilliant. If it was up to me heads would roll and I know which head it would be and I'd love to do it. Why don't we let the people in charge of Blackburn do it, they seem to like sacking people. Sepp Blatter and all of them lot, Mr Platini I know he was a good player but he 'aint very good at what he does, I don't think. I think he's useless, you can quote me on that. Wait 'til I get home and tell my turkeys we're moving Christmas."

Holloway gives his measured response to the news that Qatar have been selected to host the 2022 World Cup.

"If Darren Bent is £24 million, the game has gone mad. You can't buy a four-bedroom house for the price of a two-bedroom house."

On money matters.

"He's not maimed, he's not blown up like any of our heroes in the war. He's a goalie and he'll be all right pretty soon."

Holloway puts Matt Gilks's serious knee injury into perspective and offers a bit of sympathy.

"We still feel that we're lucky. Yes, our children have a severe disability, but it's an invisible disability and in every other way, they're perfect, and so we're thankful for that. To experience the sheer trust and love of a deaf child is amazing. The girls' deafness has touched and enhanced our lives. We're better people because of it."

On his children.

"And I think Mr Incredible looks like Iain Dowie."

On fellow manager Iain Dowie.

"I've always been an eternal optimist."

On becoming the new manager of Queens Park Rangers.

"When you're a manager it's a case of 'have suitcase will travel', and I certainly didn't want to travel with my trousers down."

"I've killed some of my cockerels this week. I like living where I'm living and I ended up with fourteen of them. I had to stand on a broom and I had to do something that took their life away. If I was soft and hadn't done the first one, I couldn't have carried on and done the rest of them. I think if we did anything wrong today, we didn't step on the broom and we didn't pull hard enough at the right time in the game to get us the win I felt we could get. So well done to West Brom. Not only did they get up, they ran off and took our female cockerels away from us, didn't they? So you get what I'm saying?"

Post-match analysis following the 3–2 defeat at West Brom that's still being deciphered by reporters.

"IT WAS A BIT CHEEKY WASN'T IT? BUT I DON'T THINK IT WAS THAT BAD. IT WOULD HAVE BEEN WORSE IF HE'D TURNED ROUND AND DROPPED THE FRONT OF HIS SHORTS INSTEAD. I DON'T THINK THERE'S ANYTHING WRONG WITH A COUPLE OF BUTT CHEEKS PERSONALLY. (...) IF ANYBODY'S OFFENDED BY SEEING A BACKSIDE, GET REAL. MAYBE THEY'RE JUST JEALOUS THAT HE'S GOT A REAL NICE TIGHT ONE, WITH NO CELLULITE OR ANYTHING."

On midfielder Joey Barton mooning fans.

"If I was in there I wouldn't try to be every-body's friend. I'd have to say 'Excuse me, hang on a minute, I think you're wrong there. Don't raise your voice at her like that, don't get like that. It's just an Oxo cube, we got it wrong and we're all in this together.' It's like the *Witches of Eastwick*. They need Jack Nicholson to come in and sort them right out."

On the bullying of Shilpa Shetty on Celebrity Big Brother *2007.*

"Roy Hodgson is a fantastic manager. The club has to sort itself out above him to give him any sort of chance. You have to direct the club together and until that takes place it will be really tough for any manager. José Mourinho would not take the job because he would understand the state of things."

On Liverpool's financial woes.

"There was a spell in the second half when I took my heart off my sleeve and put it in my mouth."

"I believe in what I am doing totally and once people speak to me they do too – I could sell snow to the Eskimos."

"I'VE RIDDEN A HORSE BUT I'M RUBBISH AT IT. I LOOK LIKE A CRAB SAT ON A HORSE WITH MY HUNCHED BACK. I'VE GOT ROUNDED SHOULDERS SO I'M IN ALL SORTS OF TROUBLE AND THE BLOODY HORSE SEEMS TO KNOW IT AS WELL! MANY A TIME MY WIFE'S SEEN ME IN EXCRUCIATING AGONY WHEN I'VE GONE DOWN INSTEAD OF GOING UP – LET'S JUST SAY THOSE BLOODY SADDLES ARE RATHER HARD."

On riding horses.

"It's one of my proudest days in football, but I've caught the bouquet again, I'm always the bridesmaid."

Holloway after Blackpool's play-off final defeat.

"Anyone who travelled up there please send me a letter. I would love to buy you a drink."

Holloway offering to buy a drink for every one of the 700 fans who made the 805-mile round trip to see Plymouth beat Sunderland 3–2 away.

"HE'S SIX FOOT SOMETHING, FIT AS A FLEA, GOOD LOOKING – HE'S GOT TO HAVE SOMETHING WRONG WITH HIM. HOPEFULLY HE'S HUNG LIKE A HAMSTER. THAT WOULD MAKE US ALL FEEL BETTER. HAVING SAID THAT, ME MISSUS HAS GOT A PET HAMSTER AT HOME, AND HIS COCK'S MASSIVE."

On Cristiano Ronaldo.

"When you see the coals, your first reaction is to think 'my God, that's going to burn me' ... If someone can teach you how to put that out of your mind, how can that fail to make you a better footballer? You may not be able to walk afterwards, which is a risk, but it's one we're willing to take. You have to stop thinking about your family or anything else that is going on outside the game. You can get better at it and the more experience you get the easier it becomes."

"He was a very special bloke and one of a handful of people I am proud to have been on the planet at the same time as. The Beatles, Elvis, Muhammad Ali ... they are the great figures of our age. David Beckham will be one day too. They are icons... In fact, when we go to Fulham I'll take a little hacksaw, smuggle the statue on the team bus and take it home with me."

Holloway reveals his admiration for Michael Jackson after a statue of him was unveiled at Craven Cottage.

"I AM MORE THAN HAPPY AND I AM AFRAID THE CHAIRMAN WILL NEED A HELL OF A TUB OF CREAM TO GET RID OF ME – I'M LIKE A BAD RASH AND NOT EASILY CURABLE."

On his future at Blackpool.

Reporter: Ian, have you got any injury worries?

Holloway: No, I'm fully fit, thank you.

"I was kicking things before I could walk."

Holloway starts young.

"We've got a good squad and we're going to cut our cloth accordingly, but I think the cloth that we've got could make some good soup, if that makes any sense."

No.

"I have such bad luck at the moment that if I fell in a barrel of boobs I'd come out sucking my thumb."

"Sometimes it's time for hen fap, and now is one of those times!"

"I call us the Orange club – because our future's bright!"

On QPR's potential.

"Sometimes when you aim for the stars, you hit the moon."

"The fat lady has finished singing and unfortunately I don't like her tune. That's it in football. You're famous for two seconds in football and then you're gone."

On Blackpool being relegated.

"Sir Alex Ferguson is a winner. He would never dream of not being interested in winning any match. That man deserves to pick whatever team he wants to pick. No one should question it. Look at his record. Those people running the game, what planet are they on? They must have beamed down from planet Zarf. How dare they talk about Sir Alex like that? Haven't they seen how successful he is?"

On the suggestion that Sir Alex Ferguson didn't want to beat Blackpool.

"Our castle was made of sand. But there's concrete underneath."

On the future of Blackpool after relegation.

"I'M GETTING PLAUDITS FOR
BEING A COMEDIAN – I'M
NOT A COMEDIAN, I'M A
FOOTBALL MANAGER AND
I WANT TO MANAGE AT THE
HIGHEST LEVEL. I TOOK A
WHILE TO GET THERE AS
A PLAYER AND I'LL TAKE
A WHILE TO GET THERE
AS A MANAGER, BUT I'M
GOING TO GET THERE."

On being a manager. Not a comedian.